RAISING BUILDERS

A Father's Letters to His Sons on Faith, Discipline, and the Men God Intended Them to Become

Kevin Horton

Published by **Kevin Horton Publishing**

Georgia, United States

First Edition

ISBN: 979-8-9951044-1-4

Dedication

For Will and Jack.

From the moment you entered this world, my life was no longer my own. It became my responsibility—and my privilege—to help shape the men you would become.

My prayer is that you grow into builders.

Builders of faith.

Builders of families.

Builders of lives that honor God.

If these pages ever find you on a day when you feel uncertain, remember this:

You were loved from the very beginning.

Love always,

Dad

Author's Note

I began writing these letters when my sons were still very young.

One of them was learning to read and ask questions about the world around him. The other had not yet been born. Like most fathers, I found myself thinking often about the future—about the kind of men they might become and the kind of guidance they might one day need.

Life moves quickly. Children grow faster than we expect. And none of us are promised tomorrow.

I did not want the most important lessons of my life to live only in conversations that might be forgotten over time. I wanted them written down—clearly, honestly, and in a way that my sons could return to whenever they needed them.

This book is not written by an expert or a theologian.

It is written by a father.

A man shaped by his parents, his faith, his mistakes, and the responsibility of raising a family. I have learned many lessons the hard way, and I have been blessed by people who showed me what integrity, sacrifice, and faith look like in everyday life.

These letters are meant first for my sons.

But they are also shared publicly because I believe many fathers think about these same things. We want to raise strong children. We want to pass on faith and character. We want to prepare our families for a world that will not always encourage those values.

If another father finds something useful in these pages, then sharing them will have been worthwhile.

At its heart, this book is about building.

Building faith.

Building character.

Building families.

Building lives that stand firm long after we are gone.

That is what I hope these letters help my sons do.

Before You Begin

Will and Jack,

If you are holding this one day and I am not in the room, know this first:

This was written long before you needed it.

I did not write these letters because something was wrong. I wrote them because I love you.

Life moves quickly. Voices fade. I never wanted mine to disappear without leaving something steady behind.

Part of this is preservation.

If I am not there to guide you, I want you to hear me. If you ever feel lost, I want you to have direction. If you wonder what I believed or how I tried to raise you, it is here.

Part of this is gratitude.

I am not self-made. I was shaped by your Papa and Gammie. By your mother and her family. By men and women who worked hard and loved quietly. This honors them too.

And part of this is hope.

Hope that you would know you were loved from the very beginning.

Hope that other fathers might read this and see themselves in it—not because I am extraordinary, but because I am simple. A man who wanted the best for his family. A father who prayed his sons would be better than him. Stronger. Kinder. More disciplined. More faithful.

Everything that follows is not perfection. It is intention. It is reflection. It is my effort to pour into you while I could.

Remember this before anything else:

You were loved from the very beginning.

Love always,

Dad

Contents

ACT III
Stewardship 101

ACT I

Structure

S tructure: the steady patterns, habits, and examples that shape a life before that life fully understands what is shaping it.

These are the lessons learned in childhood that quietly shape the men we become.

"Yet you, Lord, are our Father. We are the clay, you are the potter; we are all the work of your hand." — Isaiah 64:8

Before you understood what was happening around you, you were being shaped.

By the tone of our home.

By our routines.

By the way we handled frustration and forgiveness.

Structure is the rhythm of a family.

It is how love is shown.

How correction is given.

How faith is practiced when no one is watching.

It is built in ordinary days—quiet mornings, long afternoons, regular evenings, and the same lessons repeated until they begin to stick.

Shaping doesn't announce itself.

But it is always happening.

Just as clay is formed slowly in a potter's hands, character is formed slowly inside a home.

This act is about those early patterns.

The house we tried to build.

The tone we tried to set.

The faith we tried to model.

Because what is shaped early becomes strength later.

Love always,

Dad

LETTER ONE

Early Season Formation

Will and Jack,

You will not remember most of these early years.

You will not remember how small your hands were, how your voices sounded, or how often you asked the same question again and again.

But you are being formed.

Long before you understand why something is right or wrong, you are learning.

You are watching.

You are absorbing.

Proverbs says:

"The fear of the Lord is the beginning of wisdom." — Proverbs 9:10

Wisdom does not begin later in life.

It begins early.

It begins with small habits.

With respect.

With listening.

With learning that your words matter.

I see it when we climb trees together.

You look down carefully before stepping.

You ask where your foot should go.

You concentrate.

You try again if you slip.

You feel proud when you get a little higher than the day before.

I see it in other ways too.

It makes your mom laugh sometimes during Florida Gators games. When I yell at a referee or a player on the screen, Will repeats what I said a few seconds later.

"Rebound!"

"You need to block!"

You watch everything.

Even when you don't realize it.

That is formation.

It is slow.

It is steady.

It is built one careful step at a time.

The same is true with character.

The way you respond to correction.

The way you speak to your mother.

The way you handle losing a board game on the ottoman.

The way you tell the truth when it would be easier not to.

These moments feel small.

They are not.

They are shaping you.

I do not expect perfection.

I expect growth.

And growth takes repetition.

It takes correction.

It takes patience—from you and from me.

One day you will look back and realize these early years mattered more than you knew.

Formation is quiet.

But it is powerful.

One day you will realize that the habits you formed as boys quietly became the character you carried as men.

And I am grateful to be part of yours.

Your children will reap what you sow.

Love always,

Dad

LETTER TWO

Discipline and Love

Will,

Discipline is not punishment.

It is guidance.

It is correction given because someone cares enough not to ignore what could grow into something worse.

The Bible says:

"Whoever spares the rod hates their children, but the one who loves their children is careful to discipline them." — Proverbs 13:24

That verse is not about anger.

It is about love.

Love does not look away.

Love steps in.

You were recently not allowed screen time for a month because of disrespect and talking back.

That was not easy.

It was not fun for you.

It was not fun for us either.

But allowing that behavior to grow would have been easier in the moment—and worse in the long run.

You are passionate.

You are fiery.

You feel things deeply.

That is a strength.

But it must be shaped.

When you have a meltdown, we sit with you.

We let you calm down.

We talk through what happened.

We correct.
And then we hug.

Discipline without love creates distance.

Love without discipline creates weakness.

The balance is not always perfect.

I am learning too.

But understand this:

Every correction is meant to build you.

Not break you.

Every boundary is meant to protect you.

Not control you.

Hard lessons often need to be repeated.

Even for adults.

Especially for adults.

What matters is not how many times you fall short.

What matters is whether you absorb the lesson and grow from it.

You are a good boy.

And we are committed to teaching you what is right—no matter how many times it takes.

"I am neither especially clever nor especially gifted. I am only very, very curious." — Albert Einstein

Love always,

Dad

LETTER THREE

A Joyous Answer to Prayer

Will and Jack,

Before you were ever in our arms, you were in our prayers.

Children are not something we assumed would simply happen.

They were hoped for.

Asked for.

Entrusted to us.

The Bible says of Hannah:

"I prayed for this child, and the Lord has granted me what I asked of him." — 1 Samuel 1:27

That verse has always meant something to me.

There is joy in receiving what you prayed for.

There is also responsibility.

When we found out we were having you, it was a mixture of emotions.

Excitement.

Gratitude.

A little fear.

During Will's pregnancy, the world was in the middle of COVID. Everything felt uncertain. Hospital policies were changing. The world felt quieter and stranger than normal.

When you were born, Will, I remember holding you and realizing how small you were—and how completely dependent you were on us.

There wasn't one overwhelming emotion.

It was layered.

Protective love.

Weight.

Responsibility.

Confidence that we would figure it out.

And help came quickly. Your grandmothers showed up in ways that steadied us in those early days.

Jack, your pregnancy has been different—still a gift, still an answer to prayer—mixed with nausea and long days for your mother. But the gratitude remains the same.

You were wanted.

You were prayed for.

You were entrusted.

And with that joy comes responsibility.

It is our job to pour a foundation into you.

To guide.

To protect.

To teach.

I do not take that lightly.

"Great things come from hard work and perseverance. No excuses."
— Kobe Bryant

Love always,

Dad

LETTER FOUR

Evenings Together

Will,

Some of the most important moments in a family are the quiet ones that happen at the end of the day.

Work is finished.

The sun is starting to go down.

And the house settles into its evening rhythm.

Those are the hours I look forward to most.

I work hard during the day, but when the workday ends, the part I enjoy most begins.

You seem to feel it too.

When I finish my last call or close my computer, you're usually ready to go outside.

Sometimes we throw a ball.

Sometimes we swing.

Sometimes we climb trees together.

Other times we end up in playful karate matches that usually leave both of us laughing.

Other evenings we grill together or sit and watch the Florida Gators play.

The Bible says:

"Every good and perfect gift is from above." — James 1:17

It's easy to think of big things when we hear that verse.

But many of the best gifts are simple ones.

Time together.

Laughter.

Learning small things side by side.

You ask questions about how things work.

Why we season food a certain way.
Why we flip something on the grill when we do.

Your curiosity makes me want to do better.

Because I know you're watching.

These evenings are not just about relaxing.

They are about learning.

About being together.

About building a relationship that will last long after childhood ends.

Presence is a far better gift than presents.

Love always,

Dad

LETTER FIVE

Learning Takes Time

Will and Jack,

Learning rarely happens all at once.

Most lessons are heard many times before they finally stick.

The Bible says:

"Impress them on your children. Talk about them when you sit at home and when you walk along the road, when you lie down and when you get up." — Deuteronomy 6:7

The most important lessons are not delivered once.

They are woven into everyday life.

One thing that amazes me about you, Will, is how curious you are.

You ask questions about everything.

Why things work the way they do.

Why we cook things a certain way.

Why something happens the way it does.

But what surprises me even more is how well you remember the answers.

For a five-year-old, your ability to retain information is impressive.

You connect things.

You remember conversations.

You apply lessons we talked about earlier.

You are incredibly inquisitive.

And you are incredibly smart.

That curiosity is a gift.

Sometimes lessons come back later.

Through a song.

Through something we see on television.

Through a passage in the Bible.

When that happens, we talk about it again.

Not to lecture you.

But to help the lesson take root.

And when you recognize a lesson yourself and apply it, we celebrate that.

There is no shortage of encouragement in our house when you do the right thing.

Growth happens little by little.

The same patience it takes to learn as a boy is the same patience it takes to build a life as a man.

Even adults need reminders.

"Whatever you do in life, surround yourself with smart people who'll argue with you." — John Wooden

Love always,

Dad

LETTER SIX

Brotherhood

Will and Jack,

You will always have a six-year gap between you.

Right now that difference may feel big.

One of you will be older, stronger, and able to do things the other cannot yet do.

But time has a way of shrinking that distance.

And one day that difference will matter very little.

The Bible says:

"As iron sharpens iron, so one person sharpens another." — Proverbs 27:17

Brothers are meant to sharpen each other.

That will not always feel pleasant.

You will compete.

You will argue.

You will irritate each other at times.

That is normal.

My brother is about five and a half years younger than me.

We played together.

We fought sometimes.

But we also hunted together.

We traveled to countless Florida Gators games together.

Even as life spread us into different places, we stayed connected.

Over time I also began to realize something important about having a brother.

A brother is one of the few people in life who truly understands where you came from. You grow up in the same house. You see the same parents. You experience many of the same moments that shape your childhood.

That shared history creates a bond that is difficult to replace.

Your uncle and I didn't always see things the same way when we were younger. Like most brothers, we had our share of disagreements and competition. But as we got older, those differences mattered less and the connection mattered more.

We learned to rely on each other.

We learned to support each other.

And we learned that family is one of the few things in life that should never be taken for granted.

That is what I hope for you.

Not perfection.

Connection.

You will not always agree.

You will not always understand each other.

But you should always remember you are on the same team.

The world will try to divide people.

Families included.

Do not let that happen to you.

Defend each other publicly.

Correct each other privately.
Work toward solutions.

And remember that the bond between brothers is something many people wish they had.

Take care of it.

Strengthen it.

Brothers are one of the few relationships in life that begin before you understand them and last long after everything else in life begins to change.

"No one cares how much you know until they know how much you care." — Theodore Roosevelt

Love always,

Dad

LETTER SEVEN

Competition

Will,

Our house is competitive.

We play board games on the ottoman in the living room, and when we play, we play to win.

I do not just let you beat me.

Not because I want you to lose.

But because winning should mean something.

Junior Yahtzee, Uno, War, and Candyland are some of our favorites.

You enjoy playing them.

But you don't enjoy losing.

And on occasion you've reacted poorly when a game doesn't go your way.

That's part of learning.

The Bible shows that even the disciples argued about which of them was the greatest. — Mark 9:34

Competition is not the problem.

How you handle it is.

Sometimes you win.

Sometimes you lose.

Loss is often jet fuel for growth.

One night while teaching you how to play Texas Hold 'Em, something incredible happened.

You caught runner-runner fives.

Quad fives.

It was unbelievable.

And you won the hand.

Moments like that remind you how unpredictable competition can be.

Sometimes things go your way.

Sometimes they don't.

What matters most is how you handle both.

"You either win or you learn." — Nelson Mandela

Love always,

Dad

LETTER EIGHT

Words and Wisdom

Will,

Words matter.

You've started learning that recently.

You like to quote Bible verses and remind people when certain words shouldn't be used.

That shows your heart is pointed in the right direction.

But correcting others must be done carefully.

Respectfully.

The Bible reminds us:

"Everyone should be quick to listen, slow to speak and slow to become angry." — James 1:19

Wisdom often means knowing when to speak.

And knowing when to stay quiet.

You once got a kick out of correcting your Gammie when she mispronounced some Star Wars names and planets.

She isn't the biggest Star Wars fan.

But you definitely are.

That moment was playful.

But it showed how aware you are of what people say.

Another night we watched an episode of Young Sheldon together.

I pointed out how Sheldon was often technically correct when he corrected adults, but the way he did it created problems.

You seemed to understand immediately.

It was like a lightbulb moment.

Truth matters.

But how and when we speak that truth matters too.

"It is better to remain silent and be thought a fool than to speak and remove all doubt." — Abraham Lincoln

Love always,

Dad

LETTER NINE

Papa and Gammie

Will and Jack,

Long before you were born, other people were shaping the family you were born into.

Your Papa and Gammie are a big part of that story.

Your Papa worked harder than most people I have ever known.

His body was broken and bruised over the years from the work he did to provide for his family.

He spent many years working away from home—more than any of us would have liked.

When I was younger, I didn't understand those long hours.

Now I do.

And I respect him even more because of it.

Your Gammie carried just as much responsibility in her own way.

She worked.

She managed the house.

She raised children.

And she still showed up to practices and games.

Both of them came from humble beginnings.

Life was not always easy.

But they didn't complain.

They didn't throw pity parties.

They simply showed up every day and did what needed to be done.

The Bible says:

"Whatever you do, work at it with all your heart, as working for the Lord." — Colossians 3:23

That verse reminds me of your Papa and Gammie.

They lived it quietly.

Day after day.

Year after year.

And because of that, the life you are growing up in today is possible.

One day the life your children inherit will depend on the quiet sacrifices you choose to make today.

"The price of greatness is responsibility." — Winston Churchill

Love always,

Dad

LETTER TEN

Your Mother and Guh

Will,

One day Jack will read this too.

Your mother and Guh spend many hours each week teaching you and guiding you through your lessons.

They homeschool you.

They help you understand things when they feel difficult.

They encourage you when learning feels frustrating.

And they celebrate with you when something finally makes sense.

The Bible says:

"Let the wise listen and add to their learning." — Proverbs 1:5

They are not just teaching school subjects.

They are shaping your character.

Your patience.

Your discipline.

Your curiosity.

Your ability to think.

One of the things you struggle with most right now isn't the lessons themselves.

It's sitting still.

You are full of energy.

But they show patience with you every day.

And even with that challenge, you continue to learn quickly.

You are very smart, and they enjoy the challenge of teaching you.

Teaching someone well takes time.

It takes patience.

It takes repeating lessons again and again.

But those hours of learning are building something that will last far beyond childhood.

The discipline you develop now will become the foundation for everything you build later.

"An investment in knowledge pays the best interest." — Benjamin Franklin

Love always,

Dad

ACT II

Standards

Standards: principles or rules of behavior that guide decisions and define what is acceptable, even when circumstances make compromise easier.

These are the lessons learned when boys begin the long journey toward becoming men.

Will and Jack,

When you are young, many of your decisions are made for you.

Your parents set the rules. Your teachers guide your learning. Your home provides the boundaries that shape your early understanding of right and wrong.

But as you grow older, that changes.

You begin making decisions on your own. And those decisions reveal something important: the standards you live by.

Standards are not determined by convenience.

They are not determined by popularity.

And they do not shift depending on the crowd around you.

They are the principles you choose to hold even when holding them costs you something.

Jesus warned that the right path would not always be the popular one.

"Enter through the narrow gate. For wide is the gate and broad is the road that leads to destruction, and many enter through it." — Matthew 7:13

The narrow road requires discipline.

It requires courage.

And sometimes it requires standing alone.

In this section I want to talk about the standards that guide a man when life becomes more complicated than childhood.

Because one day you will leave our home and make your own decisions.

And when that day comes, the standards you live by will determine the life you build.

Love always,

Dad

LETTER ELEVEN

When Life Hurts

Will and Jack,

Sooner or later, life hurts.

Not in dramatic ways most of the time, but in quiet ones. The kind that show up in closed doors, unanswered plans, and long seasons where things do not unfold the way you expected.

There have been times in my life when I believed I was walking directly toward the opportunity meant for me.

A job that seemed like the perfect fit.

A role I had prepared for.

An opportunity I believed would move our family forward.

I worked hard toward those things. I believed they would happen. And more than once, they didn't.

The door closed.

No dramatic moment. No clear explanation. Just the realization that something I had hoped for wasn't meant to be.

Those moments can make you question yourself.

You wonder if you made the wrong decisions.

You replay conversations.

You think about what you could have done differently.

At other times, the challenge wasn't opportunity but provision.

There were seasons when money was tight and the responsibility of providing for a family felt heavy on my shoulders.

When you are a husband and a father, that weight never fully leaves you.

Even during those lean times, though, something important happened.

God provided.

Not always in big, obvious ways.

Sometimes it was simply enough to get through the next month.

Enough to keep the lights on.

Enough to move forward one step at a time.

Looking back now, I can see that those seasons were not wasted.

They were shaping seasons.

The Bible speaks directly to this kind of hardship.

"Not only so, but we also glory in our sufferings, because we know that suffering produces perseverance; perseverance, character; and character, hope." — Romans 5:3–4

That verse describes something most people don't understand until they live through it.

Hardship builds perseverance.

Perseverance builds character.

And character builds hope.

Not the shallow kind of hope that depends on circumstances, but the deeper kind that comes from knowing who you are and what you stand for.

Part of being a man is constantly asking yourself difficult questions.

Am I doing the right thing?

Am I leading my family well?

Am I becoming the type of man God expects me to be?

Those questions don't always come with easy answers.

The world we live in often rewards shortcuts, selfishness, and rebellion.

Choosing a different path can feel lonely at times.

But hardship has a way of clarifying what matters.

It reminds you that success is not simply about titles or money or recognition.

Those things can change quickly.

Character is what remains.

And character is usually built during the seasons when life doesn't go according to plan.

One day you will face your own setbacks.

Something you worked toward will fall apart.

Something you hoped for will not happen.

A door you believed would open will remain closed.

When that happens, remember this:

God often builds the strongest character in the seasons that feel the hardest.

> **"A society grows great when old men plant trees whose shade they know they shall never sit in." — Greek proverb**

Love always,
Dad

LETTER TWELVE

Standing Alone

Will and Jack,

As you grow older, one of the most important things you will learn is that doing the right thing will not always make you popular.

There will be moments when the people around you are moving one direction, and you will feel pressure to follow them.

Sometimes that pressure will look small.

A joke at someone else's expense.

Language that slowly gets more crude.

A lie that seems harmless.

A party where everyone is doing things you know are wrong.

Those moments may not seem like major decisions at the time.

But the choices you make in those situations shape the kind of man you become.

When I was younger, I encountered those moments too.

There were parties.

There were jokes and mean comments about people who weren't there.

There were situations where lying or using foul language was completely normal.

And if I'm honest with you, my life wasn't perfect.

Like everyone else, I had my own struggles with sin.

But even in those environments, there were certain lines I tried not to cross.

I tried to treat people with respect.

I tried not to join in when people were tearing someone else down.

I tried to carry myself in a way that reflected the values I had been taught.

Standing apart in those moments is not always comfortable.

Most people want to fit in.

Most people don't enjoy being the one person who chooses differently.

But learning to stand apart is an important part of becoming a man.

I learned another version of that lesson later in life through my work.

Earlier in my career, my work-life balance was not good.

Like many people, I allowed work to consume too much of my time and attention.

The pace of a career can slowly pull a person away from the things that matter most if they are not careful.

Over the last ten years of my career, I made a decision to change that.

Protecting balance and boundaries became something I take very seriously.

When people lose that balance, they often begin projecting those expectations onto others without realizing it.

Long hours become normal.

Constant availability becomes expected.

I chose to protect my boundaries.

I protect my work-life balance and my boundaries above all else professionally.

My family will never have to question where they stand in my priorities.

They will never take a backseat to my career.

Holding that line has created tension at times.

Some people don't understand it.

But leadership requires conviction.

The Bible speaks directly about this kind of pressure.

"For am I now seeking the approval of man, or of God? Or am I trying to please man? If I were still trying to please man, I would not be a servant of Christ." — Galatians 1:10

The pressure to please people does not disappear when you leave high school.

It follows people into college.

Into careers.

Into leadership roles.

Learning to stand alone for the right reasons is a skill you will use your entire life.

When you know something is wrong, don't participate just because everyone else is.

When you know something is right, don't abandon it just because it makes you different.

"We must all suffer one of two things: the pain of discipline or the pain of regret." — Jim Rohn

Love always,

Dad

LETTER THIRTEEN

Self-Control

Will and Jack,

Self-control is one of the most important qualities a young man can develop.

It rarely shows up in dramatic moments. Most of the time it appears in quiet decisions made day after day.

Getting up when you don't feel like it.

Doing work that isn't exciting.

Choosing discipline when distractions are everywhere.

When I was your age, I had to learn responsibility earlier than many teenagers.

By the time I was sixteen, I was working full time while still going to school. I had a truck payment, which meant I had real financial responsibility. That payment came every month whether I felt like working or not.

Having that kind of responsibility forces you to grow up quickly.

While many of my friends had the freedom to spend their afternoons however they wanted, I often went straight from school to work. It wasn't always easy. Sometimes I would have preferred to relax, spend time with friends, or simply take a break.

But responsibility doesn't wait for convenience.

Looking back, I'm grateful for those years. Working and managing that responsibility helped shape my discipline. It taught me that freedom and responsibility are closely connected.

Even so, I wasn't perfect.

Like most teenagers, I still made some foolish decisions from time to time. Being responsible doesn't mean you never make mistakes. But discipline gives you a foundation that helps guide your decisions.

The teenage years are filled with moments where self-control matters.

You will face distractions.

You will face temptations.

You will face opportunities to take shortcuts.

Some young men allow those impulses to guide their decisions. They react emotionally. They chase whatever feels good in the moment. They make decisions without thinking about the consequences.

But a young man who learns self-control begins to master himself.

And if you cannot lead yourself, it becomes very difficult to lead anyone else. People naturally trust and follow those who are steady, disciplined, and reliable.

The Bible speaks about this kind of discipline.

"Everyone who competes in the games goes into strict training. They do it to get a crown that will not last, but we do it to get a crown that will last forever." 1 Corinthians 9:25

You will not always feel like doing the right thing.

There will be days when laziness feels easier than effort. Moments when reacting emotionally feels easier than staying calm. Situations where following the crowd feels easier than holding your ground.

But the choices you make in those moments quietly shape your character.

Discipline builds strength over time. Each decision to control yourself makes the next decision easier.

And one day, people will trust you with responsibility because they know you can be trusted to govern yourself.

A man who cannot control himself will never be trusted to lead others.

Love always,

Dad

LETTER FOURTEEN

Standards

Will and Jack,

As you grow older, one of the most important things you will decide is the standard you will live by.

Every person has one, whether they realize it or not.

For some people, their standard is convenience. They do whatever is easiest in the moment. For others, their standard is popularity. They adjust their behavior depending on what the people around them expect.

But a man who constantly adjusts his standards will never develop strong character.

In our family, we have a simple principle.

We do not compromise on our standards.

That means we tell the truth.

We act with integrity.

We treat people with respect.

We are kind to others.

And we do the right thing even when it would be easier not to.

Those standards sound simple, but you will eventually discover that living by them sometimes costs you something.

Over the years our family has moved several times because of my job. The company I work for has been very good to us and has covered the costs of those relocations.

After one recent move, something unexpected happened.

The company accidentally issued relocation funding to me twice. Because of the way the process worked, I could have kept the second payment and there is a good chance no one would have ever noticed.

No one called asking for it.

No one questioned it.

No one was looking over my shoulder.

I had a choice.

I could keep the money and justify it to myself, or I could report the mistake.

So I reported it.

The company recovered the extra payment, and the situation was corrected.

From a financial standpoint, it would have been easy to convince myself that keeping it wasn't a big deal. But integrity isn't measured when someone is watching.

It's measured when no one is.

The Bible speaks clearly about this.

"Whoever walks in integrity walks securely, but whoever takes crooked paths will be found out." — Proverbs 10:9

Integrity creates stability in a person's life. When you consistently tell the truth and live honestly, you don't have to worry about covering your tracks or explaining away bad decisions.

People know where you stand.

Your standards will also affect the people you choose to spend time with.

During your teenage years you will encounter situations where honesty is tested.

You may see classmates cheat on a test and get away with it.

You may hear friends lie to avoid consequences.

You may find yourself around people who think cutting corners is normal.

In those moments, the easiest thing to do is go along with the crowd.

But the easiest choice is rarely the right one.

Your standards should not change depending on the people around you.

Instead, your standards should help determine who you choose to walk beside.

There will be moments when doing the right thing costs you something. You might lose an opportunity, a friendship, or someone's approval.

But losing those things is far better than losing your integrity.

A man's standards become the foundation of his character.

They guide his decisions.

They shape his reputation.

And they determine the kind of life he builds.

"The standard is the standard." — <u>Mike Tomlin</u>

Love always,

Dad

LETTER FIFTEEN
Two Roads

Will and Jack,

As you grow older, you will begin to notice something about life.

Most of the decisions that shape your future don't feel like big decisions in the moment. They often start as small choices that seem harmless at the time.

A shortcut.

A bad influence.

A moment where doing the wrong thing feels easier than doing the right thing.

I remember one of those moments from when I was in school.

One day I ran into some friends in the hallway between classes. I can't even remember who suggested it, but somehow the idea of leaving school early came up. For whatever reason, it sounded like a great idea at the time.

So we skipped class.

The problem showed up pretty quickly.

When attendance was taken in the next class, another student mentioned that they had seen us earlier in the hallway. It didn't take long before the situation made its way to the assistant principal.

The next day we were called into the office.

When I was asked about it, I admitted that I had skipped class. The consequence was In-School Suspension.

That part of the story wasn't the real lesson, though.

When my parents were notified, I didn't realize they already knew what had happened. When they asked about it, I lied.

My mom handled the situation in a way I'll never forget.

She grounded me for a couple of weeks.

At first I assumed I was grounded for skipping school. But she explained something important.

Most kids had probably skipped a class at some point.

I wasn't grounded for skipping school.

I was grounded for lying.

That moment stayed with me.

Skipping class was a bad decision, but the lie was the real problem. One wrong decision had quickly turned into two.

Small choices have a way of leading you down a path faster than you realize.

The Bible describes this idea very clearly.

"Blessed is the one who does not walk in step with the wicked or stand in the way that sinners take or sit in the company of mockers." — Psalm 1:1

Notice how the passage describes a progression.

Walk.

Stand.

Sit.

What begins as a small step in the wrong direction slowly becomes a place where someone settles in and stays.

But the opposite is also true.

Small choices in the right direction build character over time.

Telling the truth.

Owning your mistakes.

Choosing discipline when others choose shortcuts.

Those choices may seem small in the moment, but they shape the kind of man you become.

Everyone makes mistakes growing up.

What matters most is how you respond to them.

Telling the truth when it's uncomfortable builds character. Owning your mistakes may feel difficult in the moment, but it prevents small problems from turning into much bigger ones.

Lies work the opposite way.

They rarely stay small.

Lies have a way of multiplying. One lie is never enough. It's better not to start than to try keeping up with them all.

Love always,

Dad

LETTER SIXTEEN

Friendship

Will and Jack,

The people you spend time with will influence you more than you realize.

Friendship has a quiet way of shaping a person's life. The attitudes, habits, and expectations of the people around you slowly begin to affect how you think and how you behave.

That influence can be positive or negative depending on who you choose to spend your time with.

When I was in high school, many of the people I spent time with weren't actually my age.

Because I worked while I was still in school, many of my coworkers were older than me. Some of them were already in college. Some had families of their own.

Working alongside them exposed me to a different level of responsibility than many teenagers experience.

Those men taught me things that went far beyond the job itself.

They showed me what teamwork looked like.

They showed me what it meant to work hard even when the job wasn't glamorous.

They showed me what dedication and responsibility looked like in everyday life.

Being around people who carried themselves that way helped shape my own expectations of how a man should behave.

The Bible warns about the influence of the people we surround ourselves with.

"Do not be misled: Bad company corrupts good character." — 1 Corinthians 15:33

That verse is a warning, but it also points to an important truth.

Just as bad company can slowly pull someone in the wrong direction, good company can strengthen and sharpen a person over time.

The friends you surround yourself with will influence the man you become.

As I grew older, I experienced another side of friendship.

In my early twenties I developed a group of close friends that I still talk to today. Even though we have all moved and live in different places now, that friendship has lasted for more than twenty years.

Our group text is still active.

We talk about everything in it. Sometimes serious things, sometimes completely ridiculous things. It's honest and unfiltered in the way real friendships often are.

But underneath all of that is something important.

Loyalty.

Real friends show up for each other over time. They stay connected even when life moves people in different directions.

You will meet many people in your life.

Some will be acquaintances.

Some will come and go with different seasons of life.

But a few will become true friends.

Choose those friendships carefully.

Surround yourself with people who push you to work harder, live honestly, and become better men.

Because over time, you will begin to look a lot like the people you walk beside.

Change and time are two of the most constant things in life. The very best of friends stand the test of both.

Love always,

Dad

LETTER SEVENTEEN

Dating

Will and Jack,

As you grow older, there will come a time when your attention begins to shift toward girls.

This is a natural part of growing up. Your body is changing, your emotions are changing, and suddenly you find yourself trying to make sense of feelings and impulses that weren't there before.

When I was a teenager, I went through that same stage.

Like most young men, I was often driven more by physical attraction than anything else. You suddenly have hormones and impulses that feel completely new, and you are trying to make sense of all of it while still figuring out who you are.

The strange part about that stage of life is that most young men are too embarrassed to ask the people who could actually help them understand it.

Instead of asking fathers, mentors, or other trusted adults, many teenage boys look to their peers for guidance.

The problem with that approach is simple.

Your peers are just as confused as you are.

So everyone ends up learning from each other while nobody really understands what they're doing.

That combination of curiosity, impulse, and confusion often leads to poor decisions. Add the pressure of "everybody is doing it," and it becomes even easier to follow the crowd.

Looking back now, I can see that many of my early motivations were immature.

Physical attraction played a bigger role than it should have, and I didn't always think carefully about how my actions affected the girls I was pursuing.

As you grow older, you begin to realize something important.

Girls deserve far more respect than teenage boys often give them.

Every young woman you interact with is someone's daughter. She deserves to be treated with dignity, honesty, and respect. The way you treat women will say a great deal about the kind of man you are becoming.

The Bible also speaks about the importance of timing in relationships.

"Do not arouse or awaken love until it so desires." — Song of Solomon 8:4

That verse is a reminder that some things in life are meant to unfold at the right time.

Rushing into emotions, commitments, or physical boundaries before you are mature enough to handle them often leads to hurt for both people involved.

Many of the mistakes young people make in dating happen because they are trying to force something before they are ready.

Part of growing into manhood is learning patience.

It's learning to respect women.

It's learning to control your impulses instead of letting them control you.

And it's learning that character matters far more than attraction.

Everyone stumbles while learning these lessons.

What matters is that you learn from those stumbles and grow into a man who treats women with honor and respect.

Be the kind of young man who is worthy of another man's princess.

Love always,

Dad

LETTER EIGHTEEN

Calling

Will and Jack,

As you grow older, people will begin asking you a question you may not yet know how to answer.

"What do you want to do with your life?"

Teachers will ask it.

Family members will ask it.

Friends will talk about it.

For many young people, that question can feel overwhelming.

You may feel pressure to have everything figured out early, as if your entire future depends on making the perfect decision right away.

But the truth is, very few people have their life completely figured out when they are young.

And that's okay.

There is actually a certain beauty in the unknown years of life.

Those years are meant for exploration, discovery, and learning more about who you are and what you are capable of doing.

You should try things.

Try a lot of things.

Experiment with different interests, different subjects, and different opportunities. Each experience teaches you something about your strengths and the kind of work that gives you energy.

When I was younger, I thought I might become a teacher.

I enjoyed helping people understand things, and I liked the idea of making a difference in someone's life through learning. At the same time, I was also drawn to business and numbers. I enjoyed the strategy behind business and the way numbers tell a story about how things are working.

At the time, those interests felt like separate paths.

Eventually I realized something interesting.

The career I ended up pursuing allowed me to combine many of those same interests. In my work today, I still find myself teaching, working with numbers, and thinking about business strategy.

I didn't become a teacher in the traditional sense, but I found a role that captured many of the things that originally interested me.

Sometimes your calling doesn't look exactly like the picture you first imagined.

It often reveals itself gradually as you try different things and learn more about yourself.

The important thing is that your intentions remain honest and your effort remains sincere.

No matter what direction you explore, you will always have my support as long as you approach life with integrity, hard work, and a desire to do something meaningful.

The Bible reminds us that even when we make plans, God ultimately guides the direction of our lives.

"In their hearts humans plan their course, but the Lord establishes their steps." — Proverbs 16:9

That means you don't have to fear the unknown.

Your responsibility is to work hard, explore opportunities, and remain open to the path that unfolds in front of you.

Sometimes you will discover quickly what fits.

Other times it takes patience and a few wrong turns before you find the right place.

That's part of the process.

Your calling is like a princess. You might have to kiss a lot of frogs before you find the right one.

Love always,

Dad

LETTER NINETEEN

Career

Will and Jack,

As you grow older and begin working, you will eventually discover that a career rarely begins with a perfect opportunity.

Most careers begin with small jobs.

Sometimes those jobs exist simply to help you make ends meet while you figure out your long-term direction. A high school or college job might feel temporary or insignificant at the time, but even those early opportunities can shape your future in ways you don't yet understand.

Your attitude toward those early responsibilities matters more than the job itself.

When I was in high school and college, I worked a job that at the time felt like exactly that — a job. It helped pay bills and gave me some independence while I figured out what direction my life might take.

But something interesting happened along the way.

That job introduced me to people in the same industry I eventually built my career in. Without realizing it at the time, the relationships I was forming during those early years were quietly opening doors for my future.

Those connections helped get my foot in the door later.

What began as a simple job eventually became the starting point of the career I have today.

Looking back, I realize that opportunity often hides inside ordinary work.

When you show up consistently, work hard, and treat people well, others begin to notice. Reputation travels quietly through relationships.

The Bible speaks about this principle clearly.

"Whoever can be trusted with very little can also be trusted with much."
— Luke 16:10

Small responsibilities are often tests of character.

When someone proves they can be trusted with small things, they are gradually given larger opportunities.

Your work ethic matters.

Your honesty matters.

The way you treat people around you matters.

All of those things shape your reputation long before anyone offers you a major opportunity.

Relationships also play a powerful role in the direction your career takes.

The people you meet along the way can open doors, share wisdom, and create opportunities you never expected.

That's why relationships must be handled with care and respect.

Your network is something you build slowly over time.

You plant seeds through hard work.

You nurture relationships through honesty and loyalty.

And sometimes you remove unhealthy influences that threaten the growth of something good.

Networks are like gardens. They must be planted, tended to, and occasionally weeded. But when cared for properly, they produce a harvest that can last a lifetime.

Love always,

Dad

LETTER TWENTY

Leadership

Will and Jack,

As you grow older, you may eventually find yourself in positions where others look to you for direction.

Many people assume leadership begins when someone receives a title, a promotion, or a formal position of authority.

But real leadership often begins long before any title is ever given.

You don't need a position to influence people.

You don't need a title to lead.

Leadership begins with intention.

It begins with how you treat people, how you carry yourself, and the example you set in everyday situations.

When I was younger in my career, I didn't set out trying to become a leader. I simply tried to work hard and treat people the right way.

Over time, something interesting happened.

People began to notice.

They noticed consistency in effort.

They noticed fairness in how others were treated.

They noticed someone willing to do the work instead of simply talking about it.

Before I even realized it was happening, I had become someone others were paying attention to.

Leadership often grows that way.

It happens quietly.

People naturally gravitate toward individuals who demonstrate discipline, integrity, and consistency. They trust people whose actions match their words.

Some people feel comfortable stepping into that responsibility. Others shy away from it.

I believe leadership can certainly be refined over time. Skills improve through experience and practice.

But I also believe many people are born with certain leadership instincts.

Some individuals naturally feel responsible for the environment around them. They notice when things are off course and feel compelled to help guide things in the right direction.

Those instincts should always be paired with humility.

Because the best leaders understand something important.

Leadership is not about authority.

It is about service.

The Bible teaches this very clearly.

"For even the Son of Man did not come to be served, but to serve, and to give his life as a ransom for many." — Mark 10:45

The greatest example of leadership in history came through service to others.

True leaders look for ways to lift others up, not elevate themselves.

They create environments where people feel valued, respected, and motivated to do their best work.

If you carry yourself with integrity, work hard, and treat people well, leadership opportunities will eventually find you.

And when they do, remember that leadership is not a privilege to enjoy.

It is a responsibility to serve.

Leadership is lonely. It's also incredibly fulfilling and rewarding.

Love always,

Dad

ACT III

Stewardship

S tewardship: the careful and responsible management of something entrusted to one's care.

These are the responsibilities that come when a man begins leading a family, a life, and a legacy.

Will and Jack,

As you grow older, life begins to place important responsibilities into your hands.

At first those responsibilities may feel small. A job. A relationship. A commitment you've made to someone else.

Over time, those responsibilities grow.

A wife.

Children.

A career.

A home.

A community.

None of these things truly belong to you in the way many people assume.

They are entrusted to you.

The Bible often describes life through the lens of stewardship. God places certain gifts, opportunities, and responsibilities into our care and expects us to manage them faithfully.

A man does not simply receive these things.

He becomes responsible for them.

Your marriage will be something you must nurture and protect.

Your children will depend on your leadership and guidance.

Your work will provide for the people who rely on you.

Your influence will affect the lives of others in ways you may not always see.

Stewardship is about recognizing that these things are not possessions to control, but responsibilities to honor.

A good steward protects what has been entrusted to him.

He invests in it.

He strengthens it.

He leaves it better than he found it.

The character you built during your younger years prepares you for this stage of life.

The discipline you developed.

The standards you chose to live by.

The relationships you built.

All of those things begin to shape the kind of steward you will become.

Because one day you will realize something important.

Life is not only about what you achieve.

It is also about what you protect, nurture, and pass on to others.

The next chapters of your life will teach you what it means to carry that responsibility well.

Love always,

Dad

LETTER TWENTY-ONE

Marriage

Will and Jack,

Marriage is one of the most important decisions a man will ever make.

The woman you choose to marry will influence nearly every part of your life. She will help shape the home you build, the environment your children grow up in, and the direction your family takes.

Because of that, marriage should never be taken lightly.

But when it's right, there is something about it that simply makes sense.

When I met your mother, everything clicked.

Before we even started dating, something about the relationship just felt right. There was a sense of comfort, trust, and connection that didn't feel forced.

And once we started dating, we never stopped.

From the beginning, there was a natural sense that we were building something together.

Marriage has a way of revealing what truly matters in life.

Over the years I've learned that communication matters more than most people realize. Problems that remain unspoken tend to grow, while problems that are talked through often become opportunities to strengthen a relationship.

Teamwork also becomes incredibly important.

Marriage is not two people competing with each other. It is two people working together toward the same goals, supporting each other through the different seasons of life.

Respect and loyalty are also essential.

A strong marriage is built on trust. When both people know they can depend on each other, the relationship becomes a place of stability and security.

One of the things that has surprised me most about marriage is how natural it has felt.

In many ways, it has been easier than I expected.

That doesn't mean we haven't had challenges.

Like every couple, we have had disagreements. We have had tough conversations. We have had moments where we needed to hold each other accountable.

But through every season, one thing was always clear.

Quitting was never an option.

The Bible describes the kind of love that should exist in marriage.

"Husbands, love your wives, just as Christ loved the church and gave himself up for her." — Ephesians 5:25

That kind of love is not selfish or temporary.

It is patient.

It is sacrificial.

It is committed.

A husband's responsibility is to lead his family with love, humility, and care.

When a man treats his wife with respect, loyalty, and kindness, the marriage becomes a strong foundation for everything that follows.

Marriage will challenge you at times. It will also grow you in ways you cannot fully understand until you experience it yourself.

But when two people commit themselves to loving and supporting each other through every season of life, marriage becomes one of the greatest blessings a man can experience.

"The most important thing a father can do for his children is to love their mother." — Theodore Hesburgh

Love always,

Dad

LETTER TWENTY-TWO

Fatherhood

Will and Jack,

Becoming a father is one of the greatest blessings a man can experience.

There are many responsibilities that come with raising children, but the joy that comes with it is something difficult to fully explain until you experience it yourself.

Some of the most meaningful moments in fatherhood are not the big milestones people usually talk about.

They are the small moments.

Watching your child take their first steps.

Seeing them learn how to write their name.

Hearing them read words for the first time.

Those moments may seem small in the grand scheme of life, but for a father they carry a kind of pride that is hard to put into words.

When you spend time teaching your child something and then suddenly see them master it, there is a deep sense of satisfaction that comes with it.

You realize you are watching a person grow, learn, and develop right in front of you.

One of the things that has always filled me with pride is hearing what other people say about you.

When other parents comment on your manners.

When teachers talk about your curiosity or intellect.

Even when someone simply says how handsome you are.

Those moments make a father proud in ways that are hard to explain.

One moment I will always remember happened during tee ball.

At one point, other kids and parents started calling Will the "team pastor." I remember hearing that and feeling an incredible sense of pride.

It wasn't about sports or performance.

It was about the kind of young man you were becoming.

Moments like that stay with a father.

There are many small memories from your childhood that you may never remember as you grow older.

But I will remember them.

The conversations.

The laughter.

The small moments of growth that happen quietly over time.

Those moments are some of the greatest rewards of fatherhood.

The Bible speaks about the joy children bring to their parents.

"Children are a heritage from the Lord, offspring a reward from him." — Psalm 127:3

Children are not simply responsibilities.

They are gifts.

They are opportunities to teach, guide, and love someone as they grow into the person God created them to be.

Watching that process unfold is one of the greatest joys a father can experience.

And one day, if you become fathers yourselves, you will begin to understand that feeling too.

The days you'll never remember are the same days I'll never forget.

Love always,

Dad

LETTER TWENTY-THREE

The Life You Build

Will and Jack,

As you grow older, you will slowly realize something about life.

The life you live does not appear all at once.

It is built.

It is built through thousands of decisions made over many years. Small choices about how you spend your time, how you treat people, what you value, and what you pursue gradually shape the direction of your life.

Most people spend a great deal of time thinking about what they want to achieve.

A career.

A certain level of success.

Financial security.

Those things can certainly matter, but they are not the things that ultimately define whether a life is well lived.

As I've grown in life and career, I've really learned to prioritize things.

Family and time over fortune and fame.

I've learned that legacy lies in the things you hand down to those behind you. That's why this collection of letters exists.

As I'm writing this, I'm also working hard behind the scenes to build additional streams of income that can one day replace my primary source and then be handed over to the two of you someday.

Because the life you build is not only about what you achieve for yourself.

It's about what you leave behind for the people who come after you.

One of the mistakes many people make is believing that money or success will bring lasting fulfillment.

Money can provide comfort, but it cannot replace relationships. Success can bring recognition, but it cannot replace purpose.

Another trap people fall into is comparison.

It is very easy to look at the lives of others and feel as though you are falling behind. Social media, career competition, and cultural expectations constantly push people to measure their lives against someone else's.

But comparison is a dangerous game.

There will always be someone with more money, more recognition, or more apparent success.

What matters far more is whether you are building a life that aligns with your values and your faith.

Character becomes especially important as the years pass.

Your reputation, your relationships, and the trust people place in you are all shaped by the choices you make consistently over time.

The Bible reminds us to focus our attention on what truly matters.

"But seek first the kingdom of God and his righteousness, and all these things will be added to you." — Matthew 6:33

When your priorities are placed in the right order, many of the other pieces of life begin to fall into place.

Your faith anchors you.

Your family grounds you.

Your character guides you.

The life you build is not determined by a single moment.

It is determined by the habits, values, and decisions you carry with you day after day.

Build carefully.

How you do anything is how you do everything.

Love always,

Dad

LETTER TWENTY-FOUR

Passing It On

Will and Jack,

As you grow older, you will eventually realize something about life that most people do not fully understand when they are young.

Time moves faster than we expect.

When you are a child, life can feel slow and endless. Days feel long, and the future feels far away. But as the years pass, you begin to realize how quickly seasons of life come and go.

One day you are learning to walk.

Before long, you are learning to drive.

And before you know it, you are building a life of your own.

As I've grown older, I've become more aware of how valuable time really is.

Not in a fearful way, but in a thoughtful one.

None of us knows how many years we are given on this earth. We hope for many, but the truth is that our time here is always uncertain.

That realization played a role in why these letters exist.

The idea began to form when we found out that Jack was going to be born.

Your mother and I had experienced a couple of miscarriages before that pregnancy, and those experiences made us appreciate just how fragile life can be. When we learned she was pregnant again, there was a lot of excitement, but also a sense of holding our breath as we waited for everything to progress well.

When we reached sixteen weeks and things continued to look healthy, it felt like a moment to take a deep breath and thank God for the blessing we were being given.

Around that time I began thinking more seriously about legacy.

Not just financial legacy or accomplishments, but the things that truly matter.

Faith.

Character.

Integrity.

Work ethic.

How a man leads his family.

How he treats other people.

Those are the things that shape a life.

I also began thinking about something else.

Even though I hope to spend many decades watching you grow into men, none of us truly knows how much time we will have.

I don't know the day or the time when I will one day go to Heaven.

But I do know this.

If there ever comes a time when I'm not there to answer your questions, give you advice, or share a conversation, I want you to still know my thoughts.

I want you to know how I felt about you.

I want you to understand the values I tried to live by while raising you.

I want you to learn from the mistakes I made and the things I would do differently if given another chance.

And I want you to know the things that worked well and helped shape the life I've been able to build.

That is why these letters exist.

They are not meant to control your decisions or dictate the path your life must take.

Instead, they are meant to offer guidance from a father who loves you deeply and wants the best for you.

The Bible reminds us that wisdom passed from one generation to the next is one of the most valuable gifts a parent can offer.

"We will tell the next generation the praiseworthy deeds of the Lord, his power, and the wonders he has done." — Psalm 78:4

Every generation has the responsibility to pass something forward.

Values.

Faith.

Lessons learned.

The things we carry forward today will one day become the foundation for the lives that follow us.

And one day, if you become fathers yourselves, you may find that you want to do the same thing.

To pass something meaningful forward.

"Don't measure yourself by what you have accomplished, but by what you should have accomplished with your ability." — <u>John Wooden</u>

Love always,

Dad

LETTER TWENTY-FIVE

The Men You Become

Will and Jack,

As I write these letters, I often find myself thinking about the men you will one day become.

Right now, I watch Will growing and learning more about the world each day, and I look forward to the day when Jack will begin that same journey. One of you is already discovering who you are, and the other is still on the way. But time has a way of moving quickly, and before long you will both be men building lives of your own.

When I picture that future, I don't think first about careers, accomplishments, or recognition.

I think about character.

I think about balance.

I pray that you grow into men who carry faith, integrity, humility, strength, and responsibility in equal measure.

A balanced man understands that strength and kindness can exist together.

He stands firm in his values while treating others with respect.

He leads when leadership is needed and serves when service is required.

Those are the kinds of men I hope you become.

When I imagine the future, I also picture the two of you continuing to walk through life together.

Brothers share something unique. Your lives may take you in different directions, but the bond between you should remain strong.

I hope you work well together.

I hope you support each other.

And I hope you remain close long after your childhood years are behind you.

One of my prayers for you is that the work we're doing now will one day benefit your lives as well.

I hope the businesses and opportunities we're working to build can eventually provide a strong foundation for both of you.

If that happens, my hope is that you will shepherd that gift carefully and continue to grow it for the generations that come after you.

Stewardship does not end with one generation.

It continues through the decisions made by those who inherit what came before them.

As I think about your future, I also find myself reflecting on my own parents.

As I've grown older, I've begun to see them differently than I did when I was younger.

I see them more as people now than I ever did before.

They were learning, adapting, trying, failing, and growing just like I have had to do while raising you.

They were doing all of that while working, raising children, and navigating life for the first time.

Parenthood is a challenging responsibility, but it is also one of the most rewarding experiences life can offer.

One day, you may find yourselves in that same position.

Learning as you go.

Making mistakes.

Trying your best to raise your own children well.

When that day comes, I hope you look back on your childhood with warmth and understanding.

I hope you remember the moments we shared together.

And I hope those memories bring a smile to your face.

More than anything, I pray that you grow into incredible men.

Men who fear God.

Men who act with honesty and integrity.

Men who lead their families with strength and humility.

Men who live with purpose.

The men you become will not be defined by a single moment.

They will be shaped by the choices you make every day.

Choose well.

"The prudent heir takes careful inventory of his legacies and gives a faithful accounting to those whom he owes an obligation of trust." — <u>John F. Kennedy</u>

Love always,

Dad

Guarding the Standard

Will and Jack,

Earlier in these letters I talked about standards.

At the time, you were still young, and many of those ideas may have seemed simple or even strict. But as you grow older and begin building your own lives, those standards will start to make more sense.

Standards are not rules meant to restrict you.

They are guardrails meant to guide you.

As boys, standards are taught.

As men, standards must be protected.

The world has a way of slowly testing those standards. Sometimes the pressure comes from ambition. Sometimes it comes from relationships or social environments. And sometimes the greatest tests come when no one else is watching.

Ambition itself is not a bad thing.

Working hard, providing for your family, and pursuing success can all be good and honorable goals.

But ambition becomes dangerous when it turns into an idol.

When the pursuit of money, recognition, or status begins to take priority over your character, your faith, or your family, something important has been lost.

The treasures of this world are temporary.

They are not eternal.

They are never worth compromising your values.

The Bible reminds us how closely our priorities and our character are connected.

"For where your treasure is, there your heart will be also." — Matthew 6:21

Your standards matter just as much inside your marriage.

When you stand before God and promise your life to your wife, that commitment means something. It is not a temporary agreement that can be set aside when life becomes difficult.

Your word is your bond.

In this family, we do not break our word.

Standards are also tested in private moments.

When no one else is watching, it can become easy for small compromises to appear harmless. But character is not defined by what you do in public.

Character is defined by what you do when you believe no one will ever know.

Remember that God sees everything.

And when you feel that quiet sense of guilt after doing something you know you shouldn't have done, that feeling is not meant to shame you.

It is conviction.

It is the Holy Spirit reminding you who you are meant to be.

I want you to understand something else as well.

Even with the best intentions, you will not live perfectly.

I certainly haven't.

I have failed at many things in my life. I have made mistakes, misjudged situations, and fallen short of the standards I set for myself.

And yet, through all of that, I have been given more grace than I will ever deserve.

For that, I am deeply grateful.

I am thankful for a God who forgives.

And I am thankful for the people in my life who have been willing to let me fail, learn, and try again.

Failure does not define a man.

What defines him is whether he stands back up and continues to pursue the standards he knows are right.

Guard those standards carefully.

They will shape the man you become.

"Perfection is not attainable, but if we chase perfection we can catch excellence." — <u>Vince Lombardi</u>

Love always,

Dad

LETTER TWENTY-SEVEN

Builders of Families

Will and Jack,

One day, if you are blessed with a wife and children of your own, you will come to understand that building a family is one of the most important responsibilities a man can carry.

A family does not simply happen on its own.

It must be built.

It must be led.

It must be protected.

The world has many different ideas about the roles of men and women in a household. Some of those ideas shift with culture and popularity, but the principles taught in the Bible remain steady.

A man's responsibility is to lead, provide, and support his family.

That is not simply my opinion.

That is a biblical standard.

Leading a household is not always easy, and it is not always popular in a world that often pushes people toward comfort and self-interest. But the truth is that we are not meant to live solely for the approval of this world.

We are travelers passing through it.

Our lives here are temporary, and our ultimate destination is eternal.

Because of that, we cannot allow ourselves to become consumed by the comforts and temptations that the world constantly offers.

A strong family begins with alignment between husband and wife.

If you and your spouse are not moving in the same direction spiritually, emotionally, and philosophically, the foundation of the home becomes unstable.

Your mother and I have worked hard to remain aligned in how we approach life, faith, and family.

We may not agree on every small detail, but on the things that matter most, we stand together one hundred percent.

That unity creates stability inside the home.

It also allows both parents to lead with confidence.

Another thing I have come to value deeply is routine.

Our home operates with rhythms.

When to rise.

When to rest.

When to eat.

When to work.

When to slow down and spend time together.

Some people may think routines make life repetitive or predictable.

But I have come to see something beautiful in that consistency.

Routines create structure.

Structure creates stability.

And stability creates an environment where a family can thrive.

I love our routines.

I love the partnership your mother and I have built.

And I love the family that exists because of that partnership.

Leading a household is not a burden.

It is a privilege.

It is an honor to wake up each day knowing that the work I do supports and protects the people I love most.

One day, if you have families of your own, you will understand that feeling.

The Bible reminds us that leadership within a household is meant to reflect love, sacrifice, and responsibility.

"But as for me and my household, we will serve the Lord." — Joshua 24:15

A man who leads his family well does more than provide financially.

He creates a home where faith is practiced.

Where respect is expected.

Where love is shown consistently.

And where the next generation learns what it means to live with purpose.

Build that kind of home.

> **"Sometimes you will never know the value of a moment until it becomes a memory." — Dr. Seuss**

Love always,

Dad

LETTER TWENTY-EIGHT
The Church

Will and Jack,

Faith is a deeply personal part of life, but it was never meant to be lived in isolation.

God designed people to grow in faith alongside one another. That is why the church exists.

The church provides spiritual guidance, accountability, community, and opportunities to serve others. It is also a place where families can grow together in their faith.

Church is not meant to be a building you visit occasionally.

It is meant to be a community you belong to.

When I was young, your grandparents took your uncle and me to church regularly. I remember sitting in the pews of a small country Baptist church, holding hymnals and listening to a pastor preach about heaven and hell.

Those early experiences planted seeds of faith in my life.

As I grew older, life became busy.

When I started working, my job required me to work weekends, and for a period of time I drifted away from regular church attendance. It wasn't something I intended to do, but it happened slowly over time.

Years later, I found my way back.

Your mother played a big role in that.

I'm grateful for the way she encouraged us to be part of a church community again.

Over time, church became more than something we attended.

It became a place where we were known.

There were even a couple of Sundays early on when I filled in for our pastor and delivered the message. That was both humbling and incredibly meaningful.

Church has also provided friendships and relationships that go far beyond Sunday mornings.

I've coached Will in tee ball through a church league.

We've shared meals with members of our church.

We've prayed together.

When you become part of a church community, people begin to know you.

They greet you by name.

They know where you work.

They've heard you pray.

There is a bond that forms in those moments that is hard to find anywhere else.

Even after we moved away from our previous church, I'm grateful that I still have a strong relationship with our former pastor.

And now we are building a relationship with the pastor at the church we attend today.

I used to joke about something, although there was a lot of truth behind it.

I always said I was afraid of having a pastor deliver my eulogy who didn't know me.

Faith was never meant to be anonymous.

We are meant to live it openly, in community with others who are trying to grow and live faithfully as well.

The Bible reminds us of the importance of gathering together as believers.

"Let us consider how we may spur one another on toward love and good deeds, not giving up meeting together... but encouraging one another."
— Hebrews 10:24–25

Church is not a place for perfect people.

It is a place where imperfect people grow together.

So wherever life takes you, find a church.

Be present.

Be seen.

Be known.

Be involved.

You will not regret it.

I know this from experience—if you ever need a reality check, go on a mission trip to an orphanage in a third world country.

Love always,

Dad

LETTER TWENTY-NINE

Legacy

Will and Jack,

As you grow older, you will begin to understand something that often takes many years to fully appreciate.

Parents are people.

When you are young, it is easy to see your parents simply as the authority figures in your life. They set rules, make decisions, and guide your path forward.

But as you grow older and begin building your own life, something changes.

You begin to see them differently.

You begin to understand the weight of the responsibilities they carried and the sacrifices they made.

I've talked throughout these letters about my views on parenting, and I've also talked about my admiration for your grandparents.

As I've gotten older and raised you, my respect for them has grown even deeper.

I understand more now about what they navigated while raising our family.

They worked hard.

They made sacrifices.

And they carried responsibilities that I likely didn't fully appreciate when I was younger.

I also think about the physical challenges your grandparents have faced through the years.

They've experienced setbacks and ailments that would discourage many people.

But they kept moving forward.

They came back from those challenges undeterred.

They carry a resilience and a toughness that is difficult to describe and impossible not to admire.

I am incredibly thankful for everything they poured into my life.

For everything they sacrificed.

For the values they instilled in me.

If God blessed them with one hundred more years on this earth, it still would not be enough time for me to fully express the gratitude and love I feel for them.

That is the kind of appreciation that often grows with time.

And it's the kind of appreciation I hope you one day feel as you reflect on your own life and upbringing.

I also hope that when you look back on me one day, you understand that I did my best.

I'm a complex man.

Quiet.

Reflective.

At times moody.

Thoughtful.

I know I can have a hardened exterior.

But I am also loving.

Gentle.

Caring.

And deeply invested in the people I love.

All of those traits are simply pieces of the same puzzle.

Together they make up the man who became Sarah's husband and the father of Will and Jack.

I want you to know something important.

I tried.

I cared.

And I poured everything I could into raising you well.

My goal has always been to position you for life as best as I possibly could — both while I am here with you and in the years after I am gone.

Legacy is not measured in money or possessions.

It is measured in the values, faith, and character that are passed from one generation to the next.

The Bible reminds us of the blessing that comes from living with integrity.

"The righteous who walks in his integrity—blessed are his children after him." — Proverbs 20:7

If you carry forward faith in God and live with strong character, then the legacy of our family will continue to grow long after my lifetime.

That is the greatest legacy I could hope to leave behind.

You'll never truly know a man's perspective until you've walked a mile in his shoes.

Love always,

Dad

Final Thoughts

A lifetime of lessons rarely comes all at once.

Most of them arrive slowly, one season at a time.

LETTER THIRTY

Until We Meet Again

Will and Jack,

If you've made it this far through these letters, then you've walked with me through many seasons of life.

We've talked about childhood and curiosity.

We've talked about character, discipline, friendships, and responsibility.

We've talked about work, leadership, marriage, fatherhood, faith, and legacy.

These letters were never meant to give you every answer.

Life is too complex for that.

Instead, they were meant to give you something more valuable — a sense of the principles that have guided my life and the hopes I carry for yours.

Right now you are still growing.

You are still learning who you are and who you will become.

There will be many years ahead of you filled with opportunities, challenges, victories, and lessons.

Along the way you will make mistakes.

You will have moments where you wish you had chosen differently.

You will have days where things feel uncertain.

That is part of being human.

None of us lives life perfectly.

Not your grandparents.

Not me.

And not you.

Life is a constant process of learning, adapting, failing, growing, and trying again.

But through all of it, a few simple principles can guide you through almost anything life places in front of you.

Honor God.

Love your family.

Tell the truth.

Do what's right.

Your best is enough.

If you hold onto those things, you will find your way through most of life's challenges.

Success may look different than you once imagined.

Plans may change.

Paths may shift.

But a man who lives by those principles will always be standing on solid ground.

One day there may come a moment when you find yourself wishing you could ask me a question or share a conversation.

If that moment ever comes, I hope you remember that everything I wanted you to know is already here in these pages.

You were loved.

Deeply.

Completely.

Without condition.

It has been the greatest honor of my life to lead our family.

Watching you grow, learn, and become the men you were created to be is a privilege I will always cherish.

No matter where life leads you, remember that the bond between a father and his sons is something time and distance cannot break.

It carries forward.

In the lessons we share.

In the values we pass down.

And in the lives we build.

Until we meet again.

If you forget everything else in these letters, remember this:

Honor God.

Love your family.

Tell the truth.

Do what's right.

Your best is enough.

Love always,

Dad

Go live the life God created you for.

Quote Acknowledgments

Several quotations appear throughout this book from leaders, thinkers, athletes, writers, and sacred scripture whose words have influenced generations.

These quotations are included with gratitude and respect for the wisdom they represent. All quotations remain the intellectual property of their respective authors and are used here with attribution for purposes of reflection and commentary.

Individuals quoted in this book include Benjamin Franklin, Abraham Lincoln, Theodore Roosevelt, Winston Churchill, John F. Kennedy, John Wooden, Vince Lombardi, Marcus Tullius Cicero, Nelson Mandela, Jim Rohn, Theodore Hesburgh, and Dr. Seuss.

Scripture quotations are taken from the Holy Bible.

About the Author

Kevin Horton is a husband, father, and writer focused on faith, discipline, and the principles that shape strong men and strong families.

His writing reflects a belief that character is built slowly—through daily choices, personal responsibility, and a commitment to live with integrity even when no one is watching. Drawing from his own experiences as a father, husband, and leader, he writes about the lessons that shape a life and the responsibility each generation carries to pass wisdom to the next.

Raising Builders was written as a collection of letters to his sons about faith, discipline, and the kind of men they are called to become.

Kevin lives with his family and continues to write about faith, leadership, stewardship, and the long-term work of building a life that lasts.

www.ingramcontent.com/pod-product-compliance
Lightning Source LLC
Chambersburg PA
CBHW010939140726
47988CB00010B/3518